What I Can Learn From The Incredible and Fantastic Life of Ingvar Kamprad
Published by Moppet Books
Los Angeles, California

Copyright © 2019 Moppet Books
All rights reserved including the right of reproduction in whole or in part
in any form without written permission from the publisher.

ISBN: 978-1-7337921-0-3

Art direction and book design by Melissa Medina
Written by Fredrik Colting and Melissa Medina

Printed in China

www.moppetbookspublishing.com

What I Can Learn From the Incredible and Fantastic Life

— of —

Ingvar Kamprad

By Fredrik Colting & Melissa Medina
Illustrations By Giordano Poloni

MOPPET BOOKS

Let's get to know Ingvar Kamprad.

He was a Swedish businessman and the founder of IKEA—you know, the giant blue and yellow furniture store that serves one dollar hot dogs and meatballs with lingonberries. Yum!

Ingvar wanted to sell stylish furniture that everyone could afford, and he had lots of new ideas for how to do it—like making furniture fit in flat packages, and letting customers put together their own furniture at home.

He started his first business when he was just five years old and went on to own the largest furniture and homewares company in the world. I guess he knew a thing or two about design, business, and...meatballs!

Ingvar did something that no one else in the world had ever done—he made it possible for almost everyone to afford a stylish home. This made him one of the most successful and wealthiest people on the planet. But guess what? It was his strong beliefs, not his money, that really made him great.

He believed that people share the same basic needs and should be treated equally. He was very thrifty, but also very generous, and believed in helping people.

So Ingvar was not a typical billionaire business guy, but someone who was a good leader and used his business to create a better everyday life for as many people as possible.

Funtastic Facts
About Ingvar Kamprad

1. He started his first business at five years old, selling matches to his neighbors.

2. He used money his father gave him for graduating high school with good grades to start IKEA at age 17.

3. The name IKEA comes from his initials (IK), the farm he grew up on called Elmtaryd (E) and the nearest village named Agunnaryd (A).

4. He named IKEA products after things he could easily remember, like names of cities and flowers.

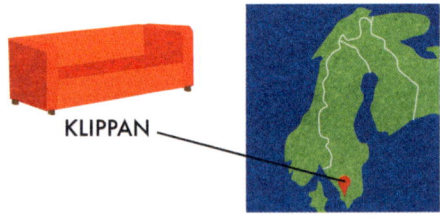

5 He didn't like to spend money on things and bought second hand clothes and brought his own lunch to work every day.

6 He worked hard every day of his life until he was 87!

7 He first launched his IKEA catalogue in 1951. Today it's printed in more than 200 million copies in over 30 languages.

8 He got up at 5:30 in the morning every day.

9 He divided his day into 10-minute units and made sure to use each unit to be as productive as possible.

10 His favorite food was…hot dogs!

Let's start from the very beginning...

Ingvar was born in 1926 on a small farm in Sweden, called Elmtaryd, near the slightly bigger but still very small village of Agunnaryd. He grew up with his sister and his parents, who were farmers, and their neighbors, who were farmers, and their neighbor's neighbors, who were also farmers.

This was a place where the only job around was farming, and everybody worked hard out in the fields to make sure they had enough food to eat. Ingvar quickly learned that when you don't have much, nothing goes to waste.

Ingvar, however, was not interested in becoming a farmer. He dreamed of doing something different. So he looked around his small town and thought, *What do people need other than food?* Well, they need things for their homes. What if he could find those things and then sell them to the farmers? And just like that, when Ingvar was only five years old, he started his first business, selling matches to his neighbors. By the time he was seven he was making deliveries on his bicycle to other villages as well, selling seeds, greeting cards, pens, and even Christmas tree decorations.

However, Ingvar knew that by working hard you could overcome anything, and when he turned 17 he finished school. His father was very proud of him and gave him some money that he had saved just for this occasion. Ingvar looked at the money. What should he do with it? Buy a new bicycle, or even a car? All those things sounded fun, but it wasn't what Ingvar dreamed of.

He dreamed of something bigger!

It was 1943 when Ingvar used the money his father gave him to start his own company. This company would do the same things he did when he sold matches to his neighbors when he was five, just bigger and better and with more things. He figured out what people needed and decided that his company would sell pens, wallets, picture frames, watches, jewelry and nylon stockings.

Now for the big question— what should he name his new company? He thought hard about it. What if he used the "I" in Ingvar, the "K" in Kamprad, the "E" for the family farm Elmtaryd, and "A" for the village of Agunnaryd where he grew up?

That spelled out... I-K-E-A.
Yes, IKEA it was!

Ingvar sold his products door to door at first, then by mail order.

His small company was growing nicely, so in 1948 he decided to go bigger and launched the first IKEA furniture line.

He used local manufacturers, near where he grew up in the Swedish forests, to make the furniture, and he quickly got more and more customers.

But selling lots of furniture was not Ingvar's only goal. Growing up on the farm without much money, he felt that his mission was also to help as many people as possible create a better life.

He thought, if everyone could have stylish furniture for their homes, that would improve their lives. In order to do that he had to produce it at a price that almost anyone could afford.

Furniture For Everyone!

Ingvar wanted to sell furniture all over Sweden, so he created a catalogue that people could use to buy from—the now famous IKEA catalogue! But because of his dyslexia, he had trouble remembering random product codes.

So he came up with a system of how all ikea products would be named that would be easy for him to remember.

They are named after a specific Swedish word based on the type of product.

For example...

Bathroom articles = Swedish lakes

Bed textiles = Flowers and plants

Children's products = Mammals and birds

Desks and office chairs = Scandinavian boys' names

Fabrics and curtains = Scandinavian girls' names

Sofas, chairs and dining tables = Swedish places

Bedroom furniture = Norwegian places

Rugs = Danish places

So even though the product names might look a little weird to people that aren't Scandinavian, there is a very clever method in place!

Ingvar quickly discovered that other companies were also selling lower priced furniture, so he needed to come up with something to really set IKEA apart. One day he watched a co-worker try to load a table into his car. But it was so big that it didn't fit. So he took the legs off and then it fit perfectly. This gave Ingvar an idea: all IKEA furniture should come in flat packages. This would save space and money. Plus, people might think it's fun to put their own furniture together!

Now it was finally time to open the first IKEA store. It opened in 1958, close to Ingvar's hometown, and immediately it became the largest furniture store in Scandinavia. Ingvar was so proud! He followed his dream and created something really special.

However, he wasn't done creating, and it seemed he had even more ideas than when he started. For instance, he figured out that when people come to look at furniture they are going to be at the store for hours and get hungry. So, two years later, he opened the first IKEA restaurant. Yay, meatballs!

Ingvar Kamprad died in 2018 at the age of 91. He kept working even into old age, and when he turned 80 he said, "I'm not afraid of turning 80, and I have lots of things to do. I don't have time for dying." It sure is impressive to build such a big company that has stores all over the world, with a catalogue that gets printed in 217 million copies in 32 languages. But perhaps the most impressive thing about Ingvar is the fact that he never let his success go to his head.

Despite being rich, he didn't like wasting. Every day he brought his own lunch to work, drove an old car, and saved money and resources where he could. He knew from an early age that there are not an endless amount of resources in this world, so we should never waste them.

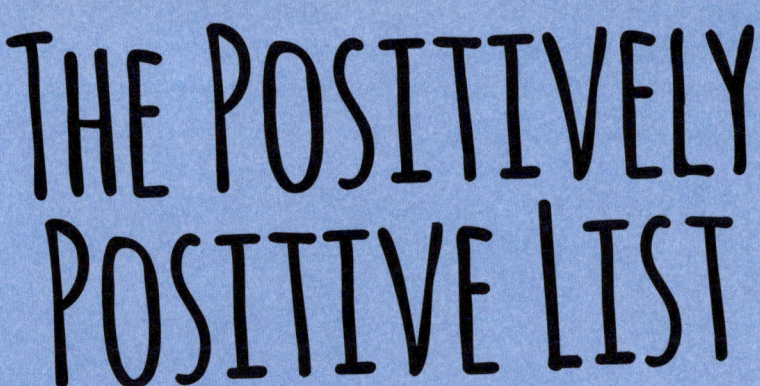

The Positively Positive List

Let's list some positive things about Ingvar Kamprad and his life.

1 Ingvar Learned from Mistakes

Ingvar once said, "Few people on earth have made as many mistakes as I have." But he didn't let that bring him down. Instead, he saw that making mistakes was a way to learn and get better.

Ingvar Was Resourceful

Growing up without much money, Ingvar learned the importance of not wasting—wasting time, space, money, resources—it was all important to him, even after he became one of the richest people in the world.

Ingvar Believed in Equality
It was important to Ingvar that everyone who worked for him felt welcome and were treated equally. That's why he ate lunch in the cafeteria and flew economy class even though he could afford to buy his own plane. He wanted things to be fair.

Ingvar Was Generous
Ingvar started the IKEA Foundation that helps build schools and supply clean water to people in need, among other things. He always felt it was important to help people who were less fortunate than him.

How Can I Be Great Like Ingvar?

First of all, you should always be yourself because you are already great! But it is a good idea to learn from people who have experience. Here are a few great things we can learn from Ingvar.

BELIEVE IN YOURSELF!

Ingvar would never have been able to build IKEA if he didn't believe in his dreams. He was also very curious and that helped him get ideas for everything and figure out what people needed. Ingvar used to say to his employees, "The word impossible has been and must remain deleted from our dictionary."

GET YOUR HANDS DIRTY!

Once you have an idea you really like you have to work hard to realize it. It's true what they say, that nothing of value comes easy. That means if we put in the effort to learn something it will feel really good once we accomplish our goals.

WASTE NOT, WANT NOT!

There's only one Planet Earth and we all share it. Ingvar believed in helping our planet by not wasting things—like leaving the water running, throwing away food, or just buying things we really don't need. And the same goes for time. We don't want to waste our time on things that are not important. Like watching too much TV instead of playing with friends!

BIBLIOGRAPHY

Kamprad, Ingvar and Bertil Torekull, "Leading By Design: The IKEA Story," Aug, 1999.

Ikea.com/history "IKEA history - how it all began," Accessed May, 2018.

Forbes.com, "The Billionaire Next Door," Accessed February 15, 2017.

Nytimes.com, "Ingvar Kamprad, founder of Ikea and Creator of Global empire...," Accessed January 26, 2018.

Dahlvig, Anders, "The IKEA Edge," McGraw Hill, 2011.

Astrumpeople.com, "Ingvar Kamprad Biography: Success story of IKEA Founder," Accessed, April 10, 2018.

Wikipedia.com, "Ingvar Kamprad," Accessed August 10, 2018.